TO THE MAN
in the RED SUIT

TO THE MAN
in the RED SUIT

poems by
Christina Fulton

Rootstock Publishing

TO THE MAN IN THE RED SUIT
© 2020 by Christina Fulton

For more information or to schedule an author reading,
please contact: mariefulton590@gmail.com.

Published by
Rootstock Publishing Poetry Series
Editor: Samantha Kolber
Montpelier, Vermont
www.rootstockpublishing.com

Book design by Mad River Creative

Library of Congress Control Number: 2019919107

ISBN-13: 978-1-57869-027-5

ACKNOWLEDGMENTS

I thank the editors of the following publications in which these poems previously appeared:

The Apeiron Review, "To Angela"

The Awkward Mermaid, "Our Wings are Proof of God's and My Father's Unfathomable Narcissism"

Open Minds Quarterly, "In the Temple of Goddess Durga" and "Medicated Musings"

Outsider Poetry, "Diluted Ruminations of Summers at the Jersey Shore," "The Conceptualistic Guilt of the In/Out Patient Scenario Involving the Man in the Red Suit," and "To Mister Wright"

Raw Art Review, "In Other News" and "How a Hurricane Reminds Me of a Vagina and My Father"

Stay Weird and Keep Writing, "Snippets," "To My Father's Best Friend and His Charming Wife," and "Quit Digging up the King of Spades"

Saw Palm, "Unwanted Nostalgia on My Honeymoon"

The entire collection was a finalist for the Sexton Prize for Poetry and the Lauria/Frasca Prize for Poetry.

for my father

CONTENTS

Sleep and rest, sleep and rest,
    Father will come to thee soon;
Rest, rest, on mother's breast,
    Father will come to thee soon;
Father will come to his babe in the nest,
Silver sails all out of the west,
    Under the silver moon:
Sleep, my little one, sleep, my pretty one, sleep.

– **Alfred Lord Tennyson**,
    "Sweet and Low"

The kind of man who thinks that helping with the dishes is beneath him will also think that helping with the baby is beneath him, and then he certainly is not going to be a very successful father.

– **Eleanor Roosevelt**

Write a book about me. It would sell!

– **My Father**

In Other News

My father committed suicide on March 10, 2011,
in Rahway, New Jersey. The next day a 9.0 magnitude
earthquake struck the pacific coast of Tohoku. It
triggered a tsunami, landslides, and several nuclear
meltdowns. 15,891 people died in the northeastern part
of Japan.

During the media machine's frantic coverage on
March 12th there was a spatial convergence in between
the vortexes of dry heaving and screaming. Everything
snotty smeared across time zones. I could not stop
crying for 15,892 people and being infuriated with just
one.

> In the blue hotel
> built from fake haiku cocaine
> I saw your lies bend.

The Transcontinental Flight
of My Father's Ghost

The nuclear mucus
of a shared pain

was the rift
between our two faults.

The Toyama aftermath
seeped in the afterbirth
of one man's arm.

It looked like yours.

Wedged in between
a cement labia
and the ability to suffer.

Were you at Natori?

Spackled to a list
of disenchanted recipients

of disinfected grace.

One man
was a rooftop washout.

He looked like you.

Soaking in the salty bits
of weightless doubt.

To My Cousin

Through time's lovely grace
your syllabic birth defects
will break both your wings.

My father spent so much time behind his desk that when I was little I secretly named it and gave it a fictitious backstory. Unfortunately, my old imaginary friend absorbed my father's final drippy and dippy moments and a new sense of adult tasting darkness soon followed. Now, poor Tony Fig Tree will always be

The Witness

The Unexamined Love Life
of Tony Fig Tree

He loved—

free floating condoms
and water glass
baptisms.

He took latex donations
and sent thorns
inside smiling halos.

Always...

looking for mommy
in an alabaster dress.

He loved—

eating trinities
of plastic fruit nipples.

His wet prize
a moment in the sun.

Nothing was holy
behind bars.

He loved—

apricot brides
and fishy beards
in wine.

His psalm number
and the way Christ
hung

with hood ornament
strippers.

He loved—

his reflection
in pools of honey
and milk vomit joy.

The way deserts
laid under him
with barren thighs.

He loved—

the way Mary wept
next to his wood
doggie-style dreams.

A cross between S&M
and sunshine.

He loved—

Himself.

How Young Tony Fig Tree
Broke His Nose

His oily ego
ran
on holy—

Land O'Lakes
confirmation snacks,

teenage twiglets,
and loose car doors.

A cousin
of the aqueduct
state of mind.

The apple tree snake
of panty raids.

Once,
he kissed
a water woman

behind a broken stone.

Her Jersey bush
in Bethlehem

told him to fuck off.

The other cheek
turned—

a trick.

A dead center punch.

The fruit juice
of a wise mouth

that never learned

to cover
his own cross.

The Transfiguration of Tony Fig Tree

Part I

(Birth)

Can you lie
about your father's
mud soaked cerebellum?

Your mother's Herculaneum dandruff?

A family
of biblical panties
and fleshy lips.

A legacy
of Newtonian tree snacks.

You sprouted
from gravity's laziness

in the shadows of David,
Matthew,
and Da Vinci's smile.

You spoke pestilence
fluently

and dreamed

of back alley sacrilege.

Part II

(Life)

One color
stalked your leather-
studded mentality.

It was photosynthetic.

It bought businesses,
vanilla church beams,

and your magic

carwash laugh.

You grew up
to look down
on Ragu.

You were better
then Peter's foot—
fungus rhapsody.

Branches thin
from shooting up
Soprano dust

in the wind.

A rebel
with no fruit
rolled up penance.

You fired carpenters.

Part III

(Death)

Can you lie
to the ethanol droplets
in your Vesuvian roots?

St. George's Dragon was bigger.

You lacked
Pilot's prestige.

Your mosaic dogs
barked
in oceanic eggshell

hues of mild dismemberment.

One look of judgment
and you withered.

Cobblestone steps
take thorn tipped aspirations,

but you skipped all twelve.

You fell beneath a symbol
of water speckled verse

and light.

He made you—

into a fine Italian

desk.

To My Father's Confused
and Empty Desk

Sambuca varnish
killed your plum-colored sensibilities.

It stained your legs
and his willow-eyed dreams.

His bad Pledge
made you gush
serotonin cocktails.

Did you get the rub?

Only you
saw a cherry wood

bud

from a day that went unplanned.

Your master left
to get coasters
and paper towel hugs.

He only came back
to count your rings,

and kiss the scissors

good night.

I read once that during a head-on vehicular collision a person's brain lurches violently forward until it smacks into the front of the skull, and then it bungees back and ricochets off the rear. Depending on the speed of the car a person may experience anything from a minor headache to J-E-L-L-O brain damage followed by death. Death always follows too close, and my father was a crazy driver. But death came by his hand and dressed him in a red suit made to be deep-sixed. Me: a black dress for a sad hippie pretending to be a size six. These are the bang, pop, and smack moments of his death and my

Crash

The Conceptualistic Guilt of the In/Out Patient Scenario Involving the Man in the Red Suit

Major Depression
leading to hotline injuries
and gross findings

does not include
four deep incisions
with electric behavioral problems.

They risked injury to the Ducts
of Coronary Hesitation.
The plumbing has achieved...

maximum benefits.

Wrist fixtures
need left artery heat
when imminent danger
visits Saint Barnabas.

Patient Signature: _____

Chris, my daughter,
I love you so much.
I can't put you through this.

Conceptualistic REMIX

You...
daughter can't love.
So much love, my daughter?
Put, Chris, through this.
I can't so much.
You put love—
through this?

The Funny Thing
About Hesitation Wounds

They speak Vulcan
with a wispy smile.

Count pages
of Seussical liability
and strangle cats.

They laugh
at pink belly rouge,
and sunset flips...

over the moon.

They like nowhere juice
and Christmas carol shots.

They are moments
in stale Americana.

They love...

just not deep enough
to cut away

from the birthday blue
heart strings.

They remember
the forgetfulness of youth

just in time for spring.

They always smile,
before the last bedtime story

drips down from Shangri-La.

Our Last Shopping Trip

I wanted
a breadbox
consolation prize.

A jar full
of ashtray tears.

A little baggie
of rolled up

you.

Inappropriate demands
for the wallet
hungry relatives.

I had to choose
fancy Tupperware.

Chrome plated
snap on freshness.

A package deal
with a stone label

marked down
to about six feet.

It was too big
for your two cents

on the subject
of being fashionably late.

It was too shiny
for your dark

head trips
into no man's land.

It was too loud
for a man...

who

      drowned

            inside

                  a whisper.

Cellular Degeneration

Your plan
dropped

dirty sentiments
into my peak hours.

Nothing on hold
but static pleas

for rollover forgiveness.

Can you hear me?

In the digital waves
of our wasted minutes.

If so,

please forward

the part of me
you saved.

After the funeral, with stanch courage,
My Mother Ate Flashbacks and everyone's ketchup
covered litigious and amoral grief.
She picked me up, while wallet ghouls
pulled at her hem.

Why did she have to marry... him?

FLASHBACK
FLORIDA, 1995 EXIT 67A

The Interior/Exterior Dialogues
Between a Mother and her Daughter

"What happened
to Goofy's girlfriend?"

Reverse gear
into a shot glass wedding.

The blitzkrieg princess
of white panties

desperately,
needing an exit strategy.

"How fast are we going?"

Speedometer mucus
eases my pain.

A Space Mountain—
sized high.

"Do I need to change my shoes?"

Little sandals
die strange deaths
in alimony green.

Lizard children
need room to grow

bitter tails
of unending

happily ever afters.

"Are we there?"

No,

but we are here.

In these postcard
moments,

before the storm.

Home Improvements

Act I

(The Architects Meet)

Splinter moments
in between
the snow globes
and missing lumber lists.

Anniversary cards
are wired
for HBO mis—
communications.

Nail tips vomit
prenuptial tile grout.

Hammer it home!

Foundations
need the lying rhythm
of defective pipes.

Act II

(Bad Plumbing)

Enter a hair
sampled from God.

Clogged in a K pipe
uterus. A copper
distraction.

Slimy adhesives
can fix anything
in transit.

Bacteria babies
can make you say,

"I love you,

Bud."

A drippy reason
to cry pink sticks.

Act III

(Add a Level)

Free range
attic women

need termite lubrication
and lots of space.

Vertical falsifications
are inexpensive.

A blue mistress
made of coke

spackled ideologies.

She haloes
~~WELCOME~~ mat
mommies

and the second floor.

A paper thin reminder
of the cost of living.

Act IV

(Flood Damage)

A septic martyr
tanked—
by his own D
             N
             A.

Soggy wallpaper apologies
mean nothing.

Stained rugs can...
NOT cultivate
paternal visions
of false joy.

Material backwash
saw

The End

of an architect's wrist-
watch lifestyle.

Nothing floats
in his fine print.

Except,
childhood debris.

Snippets

Hello...
I would like my husband's
autopsy report.

Palimony
is a nonfat spread
of indigenous lies.

You can jiggle
but can you bend?

The line went dead—
star dust quiet.

Paperwork has a tendency
to beat off good faith.

Bad faith lives in an ice cube tray.

Foot her the bill

and tag
the littlest piggy It.

"Home address please..."

My left ventricle
behind egg shell nipples.

He lived there,
once
but went ostrich hunting.

It was over easy
and well done.

Thank you for your kindness,
Sir...

but I need his cerebral

lassitude.

Everything is on teacup time.

It's spinning
into her sunny side up
Prada personality.

She bet big.

                              "Goodbye, Missus G---"

But I kept my name
piled under tissues.

She kept everything
in Cadbury foil.

No Easter droppings!

No resurrection

of *ou-er*

lord.

Dial tone...

Sometimes you do not realize just how angry you are,
until someone imprudently suggests you write

Letters and Notes

to all the parties involved
whether they're imaginary
or not.

To My Father's Predilections

Purple syphilis
is a mouse with snarky cheese.
You already knew that,
didn't you?

It creeps in all your crap
and makes you itch
for story time.

A chancre
with biblical testaments
and spotty judgment.

It nibbles on nuptials
and mediocre prison tales.
Your sarcasm melts us all.

Cerebral hemorrhaging
is a maze well met.
Ring the bell,
when you find yourself.

To My Father's Best Friend
and His Charming Wife

But first,
a public service announcement...

When Pilate saw that he was accomplishing nothing,
but rather that a riot was starting,
he took water, and washed his hands
before the multitude, saying,
I am innocent of the blood of this just person:
see you to it.

To My Father's Best Friend
and His Charming Wife (continued)

Soapy apologies
stitched up my ears.

You asked me
in the blood forum,

"What is the Truth?"

It's a dollar death
in the arms of false sheep!

You can't lie
to the crossroad spooks
with leather smiles.

You can't lie
to your tombstone
leopard hooker.

You can't lie
to my Holy Mother
of open wounds.

Wash your hands
in the urinal
of unbaptized
bounced
checks.

In his madness
you found goose eggs.

A golden cut
above the rest

and his wrist.

To the Castrated Son of Arturo's Bull

Wall Street bronze
is a makeover
for cheap suits.

Yours was red
with cherry afterburners.
A silk sunset
with silver hooves.

Horns cut checks
and tails swing wide—

eyed receivers into the black.

You perform flawlessly
in arenas of fiber optic dust.

A brass ring
nose-deep in applause.

The final hurrah
an astrological snapshot.

Rose blood on your flanks

petals
of financial grace.

To My Father's Nose

Clown noses
need cotton candy—

sky blue freedom.

A neon battery
of carousel hymns
and little hands.

They need bumper car love
and rusty apologies.

Two whiffs
of yesterday
and tomorrow.

Big wheel karma
sutured to creamy lotus

dreams of pie.

Dunk tank baptisms
with balls out
reductive surgery.

A final

flick

into a techno future

remixed with polka dots
and shame.

< *Honk, Honk* >

To Mister Wright

I can't find being born
in the diagnostic manual

either.

My father sipped
exsanguination,

after the flowers
pedaled him
to the safety circle.

Personality detox does not exist.

It is—
what it is.

A reason to paint checks
with Zoloft flavored sky.

And now...

All of my glass
microbial joy

is stitched
into his reflection.

To Mister Lukas

Your mother
was a garden gnome.
A daisy love child

that wept too much.

Her neck—
cracked

under the weight
of a sunset frown.

My father
was a stream.
An unyielding trickle

that drank algae shots
and cranberry jizz.

He dried up
in the arms
of clay saints.

They both met
in that imperfect field

where Jesus
taught the lilies to blush.

Can we visit?

Do...
we visit?

Questions
for the Elysian groundskeeper.

Dear Dad:
If You Had Been a Woman...

lipstick stains
would track mud

and everything
would be sour balls
and sunshine.

You'd be a cosmonaut
with blue vanity nails
and vomit.

You'd be a carousel
of wild plastic

spinning into a ball
of dried up
glitter frenzy.

The lost Barbie
in the tripped-out Universe

of X.

But...

you'd be my reflection
and the reason

for my plebian lashes.

To March and the Tabebuia Chrysantha

March
is two southpaw
rips
into my endocrine system.

It is an order
and a hostile verb
that stimulates
a protracted trip

into wormy moments
and squirmy memories.

My bad mood
is in double time
and makes
others cry.

As for the crucifixion
stitched
into the golden trumpet...

your perennial lies
taste like false
yellow platitudes
and dirty canary feathers.

I see you
and wonder
what a tombstone
smells like.
My father knows.

He makes love
to your roots
and mine

when March and your petals
molest my dreams.

To Angela

My father went out
drippy...
and yours
with a lurid and lengthy—

BANG.

Pisces
seem to only rest
in pieces,
before they swim
away.

Brain matter and paperwork
strewn
over a backyard,
an office chair,
and a moment

we cannot get back.

Do they understand the wet irony
that soaks up
their time
and ours?

They blew out the candles
and then all was
smoke.

We were snuffed out
with them.

We'll always remember
that red, waxy feeling
and smell
of unopened birthday cards
and used up matches.

Every member of my father's family is born in March and under the sign of Pisces. I am the only exception. I once had a psychic tell me I was drowning in crazy fish people. She was right, and I am **Still Wet**

from the soggy truth:
mental illness doesn't run in my
family; it swims.

Our Underwater
Trans-Dimensional Gateway

Only fish babies
have cosmic bridges
of toxic blood.

I drowned
in your cocktail
condensation.

You died
in my sandy bottom
drop out.

The fluid motion
of heartfelt waves
across time's pill case

kept us wet inside.

My coma jackknifed
into your boxed up
holy water madness.

The split dimension
of pruney fingertips
and bleached brain

coral good mornings.

Oxygen memories
crushed our moist
personalities.

Salty curtains
hid our dilated pearls,

the blue connection

of our beginnings.

Nobody watched
our tidal pool goodbye.

Our private moment
with our shells.

We died
in the relative causeway

of liquid carelessness
and pain.

In the Time of Pisces...

Self-pity floated
for two
very pink reasons.

The sensitive stratagems
of perched lips and

the unconditional love
of salmon-colored heels.

In the Time of Pisces...

Compromise tasted
neon shame
with extra tartar sauce,

while unwashed babes
died

in washed up
marital bliss.

In the Time of Pisces...

Sodomy
was a crab recipe
dripping

with rusty memories
of mother's silver,
Neptunian spoon.

Everything was mutable
in stew.

In the Time of Pisces...

Creativity slept
with ugly oysters
and whispered

about the horrifying whimsy

of March.

Magazine Shreds

Think twice
Professor Diesel
(Head of the Nautical Mile).

See—
what you're trying
to miss.

A few clever nips
with five
blade props

have no optional power
or prestige.

You can only get there
by sea.

Dive,
      Dive,
            Dive.

Our world is water

and hydraulic ghosts
can't sell boats

in your wake.

Key West

Tennessee
swam in butterfly vodka
and barbiturates

under a bohemian moon.

I
played deep
in blue techno
beats

of a man
who washed up
dirty.

Ernest
cracked jaws
and one smile

over green mangrove shots
and

Steven's
bloody nose

I
dipped limes
in salty tears

over years
of morning

one
popped blowfish.

My father
is a dead fish;

Bridget's
pet snapper.

He's haunting
dives

at mile marker 0.

Unwanted Nostalgia
on My Honeymoon

Rusty ruminations
seep into my saltwater
tequila moments.

Grey flipper nuns
fizzle with memories of when,
where,
and why
I called you Daddy.

Ariel chess
of squawking rooks
and kings

cannot drown out
years
of tic-tac tow
boating

and decades
of fishy familia.

Barnacle lullabies fade
to black
soundtracks

of your last joke
told at high tide.

Midnight Dalliances in Time and Space at Mile Marker 54

Finger tips in stardust
and his tributaries
in my flesh.

It's all relative
in the sea's white capped
lashes.

The little dipper
is my big spoon.

Diluted Ruminations of
Summers at the Jersey Shore

Quaalude dream catchers
create
loose visions
of mini golf
and famous
fudge-freckled evenings

on the midway.

My clown
is an octopus
that can't juggle
child hood ornaments
and Miss Trustful
rendezvouses
under the boardwalk.

Cotton Candy
on a stick
will sear your DNA
to the pink and blue PDA
moment
of fatherly affections
and
mental inflictions.

One more
time,

please!

The tea cups
know my name
and my spiraling
future self
one prize

of regret
and rainbow coin toss rage.

How a Hurricane Reminds Me of a Vagina and My Father

Screaming cats
damp with naivety
and wrath.

The churning
uncertainty
of a unified
storm front

that no one ever takes seriously.

Until,
it is soaked,
saturated,
and full of

scared
little people.

Too many paths
for it take

to trust it
and wash it

clean.

The eyes
are a perpetual concoction

of sticky Kool-Aid and
stiff blue jays.

It can bleed out
and then blow out

a soul.

Altschmerz, as defined by *The Dictionary of Obscure Sorrows*, is a sense of weariness from always having the same anxieties and issues. In essence, years of **Failing to Forget**

will end up searing your verse and all your **Other Tasty Drugs** of choice.

One Year Later:

A ruling through
three senses.

I still hear you
in the dials
of tone-deaf excuses.

You're mixed in
with the buzz
of cake beetles
and phosphorus.

The drippings
of a stone bladder
before God
and Ma Bell.

I still see you
in halos of gasoline
adrift in the atolls
of Y.

The golden chromosome
of bubble shine
tequila.

I still smell you
in strange trees
and Charybdis fruit.

The monster Ficus
of heart wrenching

BO.

Happy Hour with Cassiel

Live from the Broom Closet!

Uncertainty
starts with mop juice
and salty limes.

Lick the rim!

Where are your feathers,
flakes,
and solitary Windex martinis?

Voyeurism
lives in Scotch
Brite panties.

Change
is for channels
and buckets of rusty children.

Little boys
cry foul
odors into Pine-Souls.

Save a tree
when you wipe.

Ignorance
is lemon fresh
destiny.

A blind eye
is a liquid pipe dream—

cleaner than all of this.

The Beautiful Uncut Hair of Graves

Pink asphalt
and tire confetti
all over 95

miles of bug prayers.

Accordion ribs
caged in traffic.
Bumper to bumper.
No decent coverage.

A happy medium
between garbage
and grass stained sonatas.

Nature's bubble
wrapped around a pole.

No time to dance
in these red-light moments.
Your exit
is beautiful.

In the Carpathian Mountains
Next to Sesame Street

Memories
taste like puppet fluff
and pinecones.

The dead count
with a pimped-out version
of my childhood.

Three bats...

can be baker acted
in moss.

Garbage junkies
whisper

about the impurities
of snowcaps

and how everything
is in the altitude
of spin.

The letters

D. O. A.

are brought to you
by—

Transylvania neglect

and the sky bound
fingernails

of my igneous
dreams.

Amniotic Rain

Good morning,
sweet abortion sky!
Amniotic entrails
are for the birds.

Finger painting
with pathogens
is not the way.

So, tweet my twat
for sidewalk splatters.
The sky dropped—
their calls.

A golden line
to necropsy
and scrambled ovaries.

Exploding frequencies
of the colorful,
yet empty
syndrome of nests.

Red breasts
are only titillating
on pavement.

In the Temple of the Goddess Durga

I knelt in a golden
dreamscape uterus.

That place between sleep
and sticky reckoning.

The great hall of primordial
pancake batter.
The temple
of an eight-fisted diva.

The one woman
with a closed lotus
and a knowing smile

who could embrace
years of vanilla misery.

She burnt salt
from my lashes

and taught me
to pose
in fire.

I bowed deep
into her divine promise

that my soul
could survive

a post-mortem divorce

and the rebirth
of my

Om

Quit Digging Up
the King of Spades

Crack the bone

and call, raise,

or bet

where your souls

will settle

in the muck.

You run

into his stone garden

ace high and nuts.

Quit licking the pot

with blind bets.

Jokers wild

with no hearts

let go

of his river card!

I'm sitting this out

and praying

that the table stakes

are not too high

to fall

or flop from.

Let him rest

in his hole

cards and all.

Eight Ball Ghosts

I hear you
in the creaks
of my nervous house

and mind.

Do you still smile
with Fluoxetine grace?

At night
I see your eyes
in toilet water

and smell your scalp.

Can it all just have
a fortune cookie meaning?

An answer
to a question
that nobody asked.

A generic lullaby

and a generalization
of your digitized
and memorized

last words.

Symbolism
is that blue juice

in repetitive and haunted
eight ball flashbacks

Yes

No

Maybe

Knock three times if you're happy

and twice on the pipe

if purgatory

is a happenin' scene

and close to my heart.

The Invisible Ventriloquist and Oh, By the Way, You are NOT My Father!

Your words
twinge

with his decomposing
syntax.

The smelly paradigm
of a long dead

ventriloquist.

I am not
the equivalent
of his fetid pie.

You are three times
less wrong

about the voiceover
work
being done in my head.

Three voices
one doll

and no one
can tell me

otherwise.

**Chris, my daughter,
I love you so much.
I can't put you through this.**

Conceptualistic REMIX

(Amended)

You...
daughter can't love.
Put, Chris, through this.
I can't so much.
You put love—
through this?
You can't love.
So, I can't, Chris.

Our Wings are Proof of God's and My Father's Unfathomable Narcissism

*What I told my spirit animal,
while visiting my father's grave
via astral projection*

=|=

Our wings
have stayed the same.
NO evidence of change!

Our avionic harmony
is out
of evolution's
whack-a-mole
hands.

NO fossils, NO proof, and
NO memories of yoga
like bends
in our timelines.

It takes two
opposing muscle groups
to lift us up =|=
and into
manic fits
and flights.

There must be
better ways
to fly smooth

like the butter bugs
and dirty birdies.

They made us
complicated.
   =|=
On purpose,
 I bet.

Inordinately refusing
to let us mutate, deviate,
or even dream of changing

our DNA
of 30,000 eye
facets and one
faulty frown.

It was selfish,
and just a little bit
sweet.

Faith in flawlessness
is the BUZZ
brew that we will both
live   =|=
and drown in.

Thanks for nothing
and everything.

Sincerely,

Christina and her dragon

=|=

fly

Medicated Musings

Serendipity
tastes like minty

fresh serotonin.

Do you see me in the RX numbers?

Between our lies
and their expectations
who has the time

for side effects
that may include:

dizziness, mental diarrhea,
blurred visions

of genetic slip and slides
of whiskey gold,

dry heaving
over ray-
banned memories
of fast boats, last calls,
and loose women.

Consult a doctor
if you want a drug
dealer and a free pass

to see the man
in the red suit.

NOTES

Page 31: "To My Father's Best Friend and His Charming Wife" includes an excerpt from *The Book of Matthew* concerning Jesus's trial that was horribly misquoted on the news on March 11, 2011.

Page 35: "To Mister Wright" begins with a line from Franz Wright's poem "Pediatric Suicide." His book *The Wheeling Motel* made me feel like someone understood.

Page 36: "To Mister Lukas" is for the writer of the book *Silent Grief: Living in the Wake of Suicide*. I had to read it in my first year of therapy. I hated it.

Page 38: The *Tabebuia chrysantha*, also known as the Golden Trumpet Tree, blooms bright yellow flowers annually around the anniversary of my father's death.

Page 45: "Magazine Shreds" refers to the last boating magazine that came to the house from my father's subscription, which I tore up after his death. Like all his family, my father loved boats.

Page 54: Cassiel is an Archangel that watches the world and does nothing. I kidnapped him and threw him in the janitor's closet at my therapist's office.

Page 55: "The Beautiful Uncut Hair of Graves" is a line from Walt Whitman's "Song of Myself" that I say every time I see a picture of my father.

Page 58: Durga is the Hindu goddess that is the power behind all creation, preservation, and destruction.

National Suicide Prevention Lifeline:
1-800-273-8255

The National Suicide Prevention Lifeline provides free and confidential support, 24/7, for people in distress; prevention and crisis resources for you or your loved ones; and best practices for professionals. Please reach out if you or a loved one is struggling.

CPSIA information can be obtained
at www.ICGtesting.com
Printed in the USA
LVHW090309200820
663617LV00010B/1319

9 781578 690275